Eleanor Roosevelt
A Lifetime of Giving

Claire Daniel

CONTENTS

A Harcourt Achieve Imprint

www.Rigby.com
1-800-531-5015

CHAPTER 1
Early Life

Anna Eleanor Roosevelt was born in New York City in 1884 to Anna Hall and Elliot Roosevelt. Her uncle, her father's older brother, was Theodore Roosevelt, the 26th president of the United States. In those days, there were no televisions or cars. Instead, horses and carriages lined the streets. Gas, wood, or coal heated homes. Most light came from candles or gaslights.

Eleanor's parents

Eleanor had two younger brothers, Eliot and Hall. Her family was wealthy and had many servants: a cook, a butler, a housemaid, and a person to wash their clothes. Even though her first name was Anna, everyone called her by her middle name, Eleanor.

Eleanor (far right) is shown here in 1891 with her younger brothers and her father.

As a child, Eleanor was shy and quiet and often afraid—afraid of making people unhappy, afraid of the dark, and afraid of failing.

Once on a trip to Italy, she and her family rode donkeys. The road they were on went down a steep hill. This scared Eleanor so she took another road. Her father was disappointed with Eleanor's decision. For the rest of the trip, Eleanor hid her tears when things upset her. She wanted badly to please her father.

Elliott Roosevelt adored his daughter and often told her so. He called her "Little Nell," after a character in a book by Charles Dickens.

Eleanor lived with her grandmother in Tivoli, New York, and enjoyed learning how to ride horses, play tennis, and ride a bicycle.

Between 1892 and 1894, Eleanor had some hard times. In 1892 when Eleanor was eight years old, her mother died. She and her two brothers went to live with their grandmother. Eleanor only saw her father on rare visits, but they wrote letters to each other.

Later that winter, the oldest of her two brothers died of diphtheria, a throat disease that makes breathing difficult. Then in 1894, when Eleanor was ten, her father died.

In 1899 at age 15, Eleanor's grandmother sent her to school in England. In the United States, Eleanor hadn't been good at sports. However, because she was in a new school in a new country, she thought she would try some new things. So she tried out for hockey even though she had never seen the game played. She made the team! She also studied French, German, Italian, and Latin. Later in life, these subjects would help her greatly.

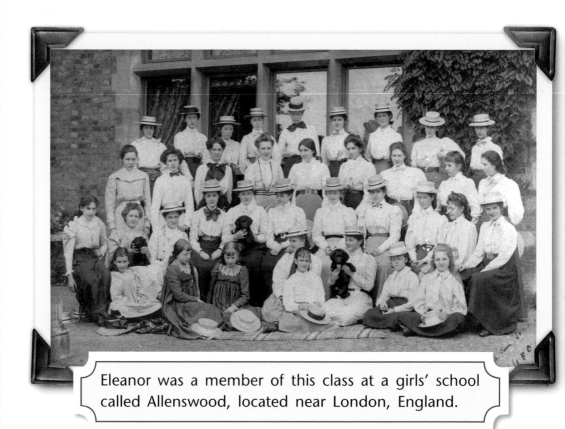

Eleanor was a member of this class at a girls' school called Allenswood, located near London, England.

As a teenager, Eleanor was greatly encouraged by Marie Souvestre. She received this portrait of her beloved teacher after leaving school and always kept it with her.

The headmistress of her school, Marie Souvestre, saw something special in Eleanor and encouraged her to do her best. Eleanor blossomed under her teacher's influence, and for the first time, Eleanor began to believe in herself. Eleanor later said that her time at school was the happiest time in her life.

CHAPTER 2
Marriage and Family

Eleanor returned to her grandmother's home in 1902, when she was 18. During this era, girls from wealthy families attended balls where they met men who would make acceptable husbands. Eleanor didn't enjoy these parties. She didn't dance well and she described herself as feeling like an ugly duckling.

Eleanor went to her first ball at New York's Waldorf-Astoria Hotel on December 11, 1902.

In the early 1900s, factories were often dirty and unsafe, and women were not paid as much as men. Eleanor wanted to change these things.

Also during this time, Eleanor began working with children who came from families without much money. In addition, she discovered the hard working conditions that women faced in many of the jobs they did. She visited clothing factories and department stores and saw how less fortunate people lived. This troubled her.

After returning from England, Eleanor began dating a man named Franklin Delano Roosevelt. They were very distant cousins, and they became close friends. Then in the fall of 1903, Franklin asked Eleanor to marry him. Two years later, they were married.

In 1906 Eleanor had their first child. Meanwhile, Eleanor's mother-in-law took charge of Eleanor's household, and nurses took care of her children. Eleanor sometimes felt like others were running her life.

Eleanor's uncle, President Theodore Roosevelt, walked her down the aisle at her wedding.

In 1910 Franklin began serving as a New York state senator. The Roosevelts made their home in Albany, the capital of New York. Eleanor's life as a politician's wife had begun. In 1913 Franklin was appointed assistant secretary of the navy, and the family moved to Washington, D.C. Soon Eleanor's life revolved around Washington parties as well as raising her children.

Eleanor and Franklin had six children but one died as a baby. They are from left to right, Anna, Franklin Jr., James, John, and Elliot.

CHAPTER 3

Changing Times

WAR!

In 1917 the United States entered World War I. Franklin worked long hours, and Eleanor kept busy with her family and volunteer work. She volunteered with the Red Cross and visited sick sailors in the navy hospital. She saw much suffering. She vowed to work hard to help these people so they could return to a normal life.

The Red Cross is a worldwide volunteer organization that helps care for sick and wounded soldiers during times of war.

The League of Nations ran from 1920 through 1946, when it was replaced by the United Nations.

The war finally ended in 1918. President Woodrow Wilson showed Franklin and Eleanor his plans for a League of Nations. The league would be a group of countries that would work together to prevent future wars. Eleanor became very excited about the league. She and Franklin both wanted a world without war.

In 1919 Eleanor began working for the rights of women. At this time in history, women could not vote. Eleanor knew that women's voices and ideas would get more attention if they could vote.

SETBACKS

In 1920 Franklin ran for United States vice president. Eleanor helped him campaign all over the country. Although Franklin lost the election, Eleanor learned how to talk to people and listen to them.

FOR VICE PRESIDENT FRANKLIN D. ROOSEVELT

Eleanor had a fear of public speaking, but she wanted to help Franklin. One of his friends helped her by giving her this advice: "Be prepared. Know what you want to say. Say it. And sit down. Never appear nervous."

In 1921 the Roosevelt family was vacationing on Campobello Island in Canada, when Franklin became ill. Within a few days, his legs were paralyzed. Doctors said that Franklin had polio, a disease that can cause nerve damage. Eleanor suddenly became Franklin's caretaker as well as his wife.

After such a serious setback, most people would have retired from work. However, both Franklin and Eleanor felt it was better for Franklin to remain as active as he could. Franklin learned to use crutches. He traveled to Warm Springs, Georgia and swam in warm waters to help him gain strength. He exercised and even learned how to drive a car with hand controls.

Eleanor and Franklin traveled often to Warm Springs, Georgia, following his illness.

THE FIRST LADY OF NEW YORK

In 1928 Franklin ran for governor of New York. Despite his poor health, he won the election.

Franklin then realized he wanted to know what people in his state needed. Because it was difficult for him to move around, he asked Eleanor to be his eyes and ears.

Eleanor traveled everywhere with her husband during his campaign.

Eleanor visited the sick in a New York hospital.

Eleanor visited prisons and hospitals across the state. She saw sick and mentally ill patients. She looked to see if patients were eating well and if there were enough beds. She told her husband what she saw on her trips. As governor, he could help people.

CHAPTER 4

Life as First Lady

THE DEPRESSION

In 1932 the United States was in the middle of a serious depression. People couldn't find work, and many families were hungry. There were no jobs, and the country was in trouble. Franklin thought he could help.

Franklin ran for president of the United States and was elected. From the beginning of his term, he thought of new ideas to help the nation. Eleanor continued to travel around the country, acting as Franklin's eyes and ears.

Eleanor Roosevelt brought grace and dignity to the role of first lady, or wife of the president. She also became a spokesperson for the rights and needs of poor people.

Eleanor Roosevelt visited coal miners in places like West Virginia and Ohio

Eleanor went to West Virginia, where coal miners were on strike because they wanted better pay. The situation was bad since many men hadn't worked in years. Families lived in tents, even during the cold winter months. People were sick and had no doctors. While there, Eleanor took action and helped establish a clinic. She also raised money to move families into houses.

Franklin, Eleanor, and their son James are shown here on Franklin's first day as president in March 1933.

In 1933 Franklin worked to help people who had lost their jobs during the depression. The government lent money to the states, and the states hired people to work. Schools and bridges were built along with hospitals and recreation areas. Many people went back to work. Franklin was a popular president because now people had food on their tables and roofs over their heads.

BACK TO WAR

Franklin was in his second term as president when war began in Europe again. Germany, which was led by Adolf Hitler, threatened all of Europe. Then in 1941, Japan attacked Pearl Harbor, a U.S. naval base in Hawaii. The United States then entered World War II.

World War II was difficult for Eleanor because her husband was often away on business and her sons were away fighting. Eleanor kept busy, though, by visiting U.S. soldiers overseas.

The United States entered the World War II after the Japanese bombed Pearl Harbor.

VISITING THE TROOPS

First Eleanor visited England to see how women were helping with the war effort. While she was there, she talked to soldiers and asked them for their loved ones' addresses back home. When she returned home, she wrote letters to the soldiers' families.

The South Pacific

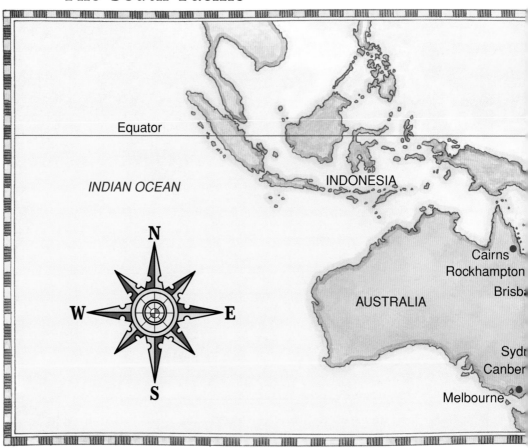

In 1943 Eleanor visited soldiers in the South Pacific. She visited hospitals and cheered up the soldiers everywhere she went. She gave them hope and encouraged them by telling them that they were serving their country well.

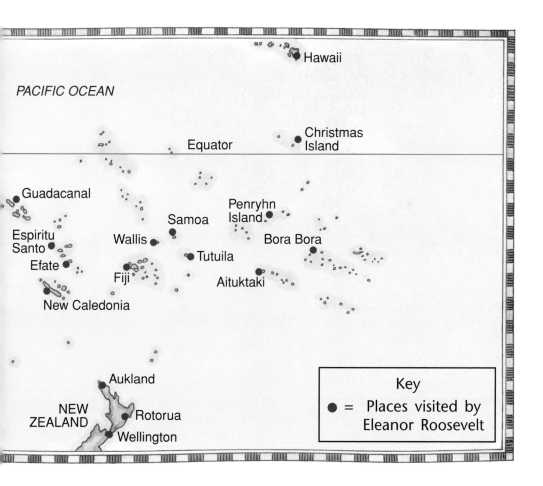

In 1944 Eleanor traveled to the Caribbean and South America. As on her other trips, she visited lonely soldiers and collected the names and addresses of their family members. When she returned home, she contacted the soldiers' families.

Eleanor cared a great deal about the soldiers fighting in WWII. She exchanged letters with many of them, acting as their pen pal.

THE END OF THE WAR

In 1945 World War II finally ended. Franklin was in his fourth term as president. As he had done in the past, he made a trip to Warm Springs, Georgia, to swim in the warm waters. However, Eleanor decided to stay behind in Washington, D.C. On April 12, 1945, she heard the sad news that her husband of forty years had died.

This portrait of Franklin was never finished because he died unexpectedly in Warm Springs, Georgia.

CHAPTER 5

Life After the White House

Following her husband's death, and even though she was no longer first lady, Eleanor wanted to keep working to help others.

She continued to travel, write, and help people less fortunate than she was. She also kept writing a daily newspaper column that she had written since 1936.

Eleanor followed her husband's coffin to the Capitol. Franklin was buried in Hyde Park, NY.

Nine months after Franklin died, President Harry Truman called Eleanor. He wanted her to be a delegate, or representative, to the United Nations.

Eleanor didn't feel qualified to be a U.N. delegate, but she accepted the job and worked with the Commission on Human Rights. The group's task was to write a Bill of Rights for people of all countries. Eleanor was the perfect person to work on this bill because she believed that everyone—male, female, any race, any color—should have the same rights.

Eleanor was elected by the other members of the Commission of Human Rights to be the Chairperson, or leader of the group.

CHAIRMAN

Eleanor considered her work on the Universal Declaration of Human Rights to be her biggest accomplishment.

Not everyone in the group believed these same things. Some countries thought that they shouldn't give all children a free education. The group worked long and hard, and in 1948 they finally had a bill that most countries agreed upon.

Eleanor Roosevelt continued to work for the United Nations until 1953. After that she traveled all over the world meeting with many countries' leaders. They respected what she had to say. She never grew tired of talking about the rights of the poor, the rights of women, or the rights of people of different races. She discussed peace between nations. After all, Eleanor wanted a better world for *all* people.

Eleanor Roosevelt spoke with Nikita Khrushchev, the leader of the Soviet Union, several times.

Between 1952 and 1962, Eleanor met with leaders from all over the world. She spoke with them about freedom and human rights. She visited countries that had been destroyed by World War II. The frightened little girl that she once was had become a woman who spread good will and peace.

On November 7, 1962, at the age of 78, Eleanor Roosevelt died in New York City. She was buried at Springwood, the family home near Hyde Park, New York. Eleanor was loved and respected, and people around the world were saddened by her death. A lifetime of giving had come to an end.

Eleanor and Franklin D. Roosevelt are buried next to one another.

"You gain strength, courage and confidence by every experience in which you really stop to look fear in the face. You are able to say to yourself, 'I have lived through this horror. I can take the next thing that comes along. You must do the thing you think you cannot do."

— Eleanor Roosevelt

Index